SOULFUL GROUP

Richard C. Bower is B
into one. Born in Man
holds a BSc in Social S
he has been a writer *all*
much hidden until 2015
started to prolifically sha ... musings through his social
media presence. His mother had passed away, suddenly with
cancer, and his bereavement counsellor encouraged him to
write a journal to express his emotions. When the counsellor
read the journal, she asked if he had ever shown anyone else
his writing - she strongly encouraged him to do so. Thus,
Bower see's the emergence of his writing as his Mums passing
gift to him. In this debut collection, Bower captures the
atmosphere of 'eternal recurrence' and announces himself
through 55 micronarratives which are romantic, classic,
traditional and timeless. The order of this book is
chronological, thereby giving the reader an insight into his
journey. This truly diverse and talented writer has, in a short
space of time, performed his poetry across the United
Kingdom – including several festivals, where he has
performed alongside fellow notable poets. He has been
recognised and acknowledged by Nottinghamshire County
Council as one of the area's most prominent writers and
poets, culminating in his appearance at several
Nottinghamshire County Council events over the summer of
2015. His poetry is being critiqued in classrooms around
Europe; being compared alongside the classical works of
Dylan Thomas and Ted Hughes. Bower can be booked for
freelance writing projects, workshops and spoken word
performances through the Soulful Group. His next book is
due for release in late 2018 entitled 'Nature' and his third
book entitled 'Sanctuary' will be released in 2019.

Postmodern

RICHARD C. BOWER

Postmodern.

First Published in 2018 by Soulful Group – *a small publishing house with a big purpose.*

www.soulfulgroup.com

Original cover drawing by Richard C. Bower (aged 15). Adapted cover drawing by Natalie Mosley.

ISBN-13: 978-19998104-2-9

'An Insight Into The Cover'

The drawing is unique. It stirs intrigue. The colour
blocking naturally draws the eye in. Through its
execution it creates an impression of a man, clothed, but
when you look closer he is actually a naked form. It's
symbolic - a representation of someone laid bare, which
is what you will find as you peel back the layers, and each
page of this book. Inside you will find the real Richard C.
Bower - exposed and stripped to the core.

To my Mum

X

"Roaring dreams take place in a perfectly silent mind. Now that we know this, throw the raft away"

- Jack Kerouac

CONTENTS

OSCILLATIONS

Currents keep reaching, taking me back, into the past -
the flooding is devastating.
I am submerged, cut off from the rest of civilisation –
by rail and by road, so to speak.
Up here in the headlands
the ebb and flow of the floodwater is intricately linked with
time,
with memory and expectation -
these unstable oscillations
have been going on long enough to qualify as a trend,
there's no pleasant gentle rise in temperature
but swings between extremes – of weather with droughts,
heavy rain and strong winds.
Up in the highland
it's only worse and more muddled.
Then the increasingly unstable jet-stream flipped again
and the monsoon rains began -
Flood alerts prevail ... one of the wettest winter months
the crops were simply washed out of the ground ...
I remember the visions of those lost
who had roped themselves to the nearest passer by
to try to keep upright in the gales,
whilst both waving and drowning ...
What followed is what felt like the worst winter freeze for
years.
But then, in time, the currents reach me -
Propelling me forward into the future,
Of what was the warmest of spring months ...

THE RESILIENCE OF NATURE

One winter afternoon, as I occasionally find,
I was wandering through the sinuous woods -
The melancholy I felt walking among the great fallen trees
was sometimes balanced by a frisson of excitement –
A desire that something wonderful would be cultivated
and was happening underneath, inside the green chaos
Out of a clear blue sky, it began to pour far and wide
The rain was ferocious, spattering off the golden leaves in
silver jets,
the whole wood began to change colour, the trunks cuming to
slate grey ...
A vision – of next year's beech-buds glistening like glazed fruit
-
I find myself huddled under the nearest Holly,
realising I'd gone to ground next to the remains of a Dear
departed
What once was a great mighty solid tree
had years earlier been split open by a lightning strike,
waspes had nested in the hollow gash,
then it was toppled in a storm ...
And now this gigantic form
lay prostate, all modest on the ground
And it was liquefying in front of my eyes -
The rain was hammering drills of water at the already rotting
trunk
And flakes of bark, fungal ooze,
Scorched sediment from the lightning-charred heartwood,
Had begun to drip on to the woodland floor
Inherent, the dense arboreal morn (sic)
Peering out from my bush, I was mesmerised –
I was witnessing the dissolution of a tree
But also what felt like the beginning of something new
The elements of life returning to the vessel
The alchemy wrought by the storm, a precursor

That changed my whole view of life – such is the resilience of nature.

GOOD NIGHT

Black is night's cape
Inferno it encapsulates
Until banging her drums
Dawn screams as she comes
Abrupt and so certain, a pure relentless momentum
I'm kicked and I'm torn, I am totally beaten
This rhythm of life leaves me yearning
Dark evil inferno of night.

Goodnight.

DROWNING IN EXCESS

An old house
it sits empty
with
nothing inside
but
the darkness and
solitude
of a cold
hungry mind
- it's preoccupied,
working overtime,
until it drowns
in the floods
that
were caused
by the streams
of one
thinking
too much.

CHANGE THE CHANNEL

Act, speak and talk

with voices of change -

Fiscal economy, the

currency of exchange,

For an active ideology

in which artists engage.

THE MEANING OF CHTHONIC UPRISING

The young man DREAMs OF HIS mother
AWAKE, AND
ALONE BENEATH THE STARRED NIGHT,
JUST AS SUCH THE
DAUGHTER WAKES UP - ALL
HEART broken
FROM FALLING IN SLEEP
OR DEPRIVED OF WHICH, AND ALSO NO MORE
tHE father WHO STRUGGLES TO SLEEP,
SO SAD - THIS HE WILL ALWAYS REMAIN
NO COMPANY TO KEEP
JUST THE MEMORY AND HER NAME ...
... SAT. a GIN IN glass
PRECIPITOUS, WHILST FALLING SO DEEP
LIFE IN THE BALANCE OF HIS OLD, FUNEREAL,
SHAKEN HANDS
BUT THE CHILDREN HOLD HIM IN TRUST
TO PROTECT ANY FALL, THAT HE MUST
MOTHER MUST SEE WITH HIS EYES
IF NOT their lives WILL PASS BLIND, THE SPIRIT WILL
DIE IF HE'S DUST
THE VISION PERSISTS IN THE EYES OF HIS,
DESPITE THE CONDITION, SO VICIOUS A SIGHT
THAT HER BODY LEFT IN
NOW IT'S AMONGST US, KILLING, AND SO
COMMON IT SEEMS
At night HE TRIES BUT SLEEP SUBSIDES
EMOTIONS CONTRIVE LIKE OCEANS' HIGH TIDES
TREADING DEEP WATER JUST TO KEEP
YOUR HEAD HIGH, THE CURRENT STREAMS
WITHIN THESE DREAMS,
hEAR STRONG ROAR! OF THE TIDE

ALERT DANGER! ASHORE AS ALL ARE FLUNG AND
CAST ASIDE, IN STRONG HEAVY WAVES
WRECKED ALL BATTERED AND BRUISED
WHILST SOME ARE TAKEN AWAY ...
... AND READING HER MIND LIKE THE WORKS OF
A FINE FORMER GREAT
SO VAST AND SO RICH, mUM'S DETAIL PERSISTS
FORMING IMAGES OF WHICH WE MUST TELL
THE CHILDREN ALL STORIES AND INHERENT
WITHIN OF THE FATE THAT IS DISPLAYED IN THE
DREAMS WE ALL HAVE
THATS THE MAGIC OF A WIFE, A MOTHER, AND
NAN
CASTING A
SPELL, HER SPIRIT LIVES ON ...
... and The FATHER draws comparisons to the world he
NOW sees
through eyes NO LONGER JADED,
WITH VISION
NO LONGER CAPSIZED

THE TICKING OF THE CLOCK

The ticking of the clock
Is like an echo through time
A single moment recurs eternal
As of those when the clock stops ticking
Striking
As one's Mother lays dying

All are obsessions in this life
In the aftermath of untimely death
Grief pervades the death sentence
It tortures those decisions with fatal significance
Haunting
With a truthful and emotional experience

Showing minds attempting to make loops back in time
To avoid the future
In the often unbearable, intolerable present moment
Time disintegrates
An experience of insomnia, hallucinations and self-medication

Of substance, in thinking

Deeper, while sinking

Falling further
In
To

SLEEP.
Preceded by a lyrical narrative of despair

An imagery replete with holes
Of the physical and from those absent
Loved ones left lost

Distance measured through changing seasons -
The pounding of the rain, the searing heat -
Inside the grieving mind
Evocative detail offers solace
Such bittersweet imagination, both
A strength and weakness ...
Its most moving, so powerfully urging -
Much beauty is seized from the bleakest of landscapes,
Light is always portrayed
Even at the end of the very darkest day

DREAM GIFT

I see Mum in many a dream
Wintertime on Headlands frost lawn
I break down & embrace her lost soul
like a young Son
Mums presence fresh, yet wise and other-worldly
Through the tears
we neither speak
Time flies as emotions peak
Our eyes embrace -
A Mum comforts her lost Son
and then in a flicker of an eye,
as in her rapid loss of life,
the moments gone.

VOICES

You call my name
like voices
in the back of the brain
that hang
in limbo,
like a shadow
and suffocate
as they remain.

THE ANIMALS COME OUT AT NIGHT

A change in shift
As night kicks in
All lights are off
And shadows gone

ALONE

Alone
as life goes
there's nobody else
just me
and the trees
stood solemn in the breeze
even my shadow leaves
when it's
darkness

EARLY MORNINGS

Early mornings crossing landscapes far from home
Country fields and fences spool past us,
Herds of fresians, rocketing turtledoves,
Vast, cavernous rocks and of spring water showers
Heavy rain-laden clouds
Lightening their load and
Unfurling from above
Onto ploughed winter fields trodden all around us…
Into what become pictorial guides and narrative
Forming imagery of the senses
Returning in, as such, these bittersweet memories –
Like the sun-ripened glow and tint on poisonous inedible
berries
As I reminisce… life … its
Juxtaposition of surreal realities...
I'm indulged as I rejoice through the
Landscape of my memories…

THE ETERNAL EMBRACE

Callow delights yet more potent n raunchy - more
vital and more RAW
The fragmentation of an image
Immortality of the beauty and the
melancholy encore
A masterpiece - painted by finest horse hair
Full of wit, full of promise, full of colour,
full of verve
An antithesis, like SINKING to the bottom of the ocean and
finding a PEARL!
... and then rising, resurfacing with a kick -
A heart-beating, tub-thumping inspiration
Returning all a-flutter
with life's very affirmation
Writing 'til late of all the
hope and all
a-flourish
Of traditional satisfactions
just as time once had promised
Momentous and
meaningful
A passion so dazzling
The amazing grace of a woman
Seen through the vision of new eyes
Causing a posturing
where one usually loses their edge
Writing of life and ideas
where suns had once set
Burning brightly in style like a beacon
A shape taking form cuts through the
night curtain
A light so bright and so brilliant, the
former storm - no longer a certain
Channelling deep dissident waters

highly refined and hydrating
Bringing joy to the surface, the eternal embrace of feeling -
Life - as it returns to the vessel ... that is the magic of sourcing a crystal, a diamond - a rare jewel!

BRAVE NEW WORD

When respect is slighted and vision blurred -
To all detritus
When one's word goes unheard -
The masses go wild over vacuous inane characters,
Whilst brilliance remains hidden
A gem - a foreign language to all the trash
Little more than a cult favourite,
Known only to a select gang -
Then, a movement in the darkness, at long last
Moves out of the shadows,
Is quietly cast
No longer forgotten... Enters the Pantheon,
Now has reason to exist...
The mocked and the ridiculed,
ALL have something to share
A subject,
Of substance - not to go unheard,
A heart that BEATS, a heart with passion
An individual, no longer held ransom
whilst WASTED!
All alone, internal -
As a tree,
An individual, not to fall in the forest
Like a tragedy - a BEAUTIFUL sunset, a gorgeous
symphony...
Both rare and precious
That passes by unwitnessed
A lofty intrigue - something special,
Something unique,
Pulling the strings, behind the scenes...
...The footsteps on the beach
Translate a language, translate a rhythm -
They transcend a beat...
When

One's moment in Life
Is at
One's feet

SOMETHING INSIDE IS ALIVE

Floating adrift in all too familiar waters
The face
Cast all naked and helpless -
A piercing and perpetual stubbornness
A furtive look
The physical, the personal, ALL emotionally
RAVAGED
Whilst desperately drifting
Yet writing... and embracing...
...with appropriate tenderness...
In the mirror - the enshrouding darkness
Reflect sharp razor light eyes like those of
SAVAGES
Haunting - the Human pathos
Glistening images of daydream wishes
Lamenting the decline
Heartened and Heartbroken -
Through intent and life's callous licentiousness ...
Resurfacing with conviction -
A figure of determination,
The sheer magnificence,
Reflecting a serious intention
Replete with dual sensibility -
A mentality
No longer of loneliness, one in mere isolation
A reason of existence, as in the first instance -
A place
No longer buried beneath the night
A STRONG heart beating within,
It penetrates and breaks through the ice -
Something Inside is Alive...

One SHINE's
In the flow

Of the bright warm waters
And the Ocean's moonlight -
No longer cast adrift,
All alone in the night

PRIMED LIKE AN EDACIOUS VULTURE

A vision, an image -
Both romantic and poetic
One borne of compassion,
Is nurtured - it surges...
A natural and magical composition
Two minds collide -
A rare beauty in life
PRIMED
With an urge and hunger
Like an edacious vulture -
Two lovers
Intent on catching their prey
Circle, then SWOOP and
Forge a path
Through the Sun-swollen grain

THE ANIMAL WITHIN

The wild tethered animal inside
Creeps around
like a creature of the night
An imperceptible force
trying to find a way with an
urge... both insatiable and immediate
Beneath an exterior of naked negations -
A shocking sense of imagery and of
implicit affirmations
Full of flight and full of fancy,
Stimuli
Towards the self-destructive
Colluding all and yet expulsive
Taken on a journey to wild, all-out darkened places
Madness is not a disease
But a mystical opposition, an active rebellion
Just trying to find a release
From the dominant materialist mainstream
Of a drive that can't be fixed by the
trap of conformity...
In a world and culture that absorbs us...

Like a finely tuned concerto,
the aim is to be particular,
to walk through a landscape... connect...
and leave a set of footsteps

THE ART OF LOSING YOUR MIND

Walk in the silent darkness
Where internal voices encapsulate and surround us
Where lives fragment, shapes waver, and worlds fall away
We go to a place where others can't follow...
When you lose your mind - where is it to be found?
When life has been dismantled, you find yourself broken and
lost -
To inhabit that desolate place, one of all-out self-loss -
An experience that's all around us, ONE amongst us and
inside us...
To be stuck in a loop of distress
A living nightmare, when one is awake and yet buried
There is so much loss, so much sorrow
An existential scariness, an infinite strangeness -
both harrowing and touching...
These attempts to endure the storm... describe an internal
experience -
A literal translation of the psychological, where your identity
disappears
Just like ice melting away, into an increasingly shadowy
interior
Language slips, words don't fit
Here, there - a face with no name
A tragic loss, a looming fog... are all that remain
But then - an alluring thought!
The movement in the darkness
Has a trigger, has a spark...
Damage can offer enlightenment
A profound loss - a consolation
Mad people can see the world in ways that the sane are blind
to
ILLUMINATING
The human condition...
Sliding away from the buzz that enraptured,

Where shapes wavered and boundaries ruptured -
A former drama made up of fragments,
One now joins together
No longer a clown in the circus,
One is now the ceremonial conductor
No longer dancing to a different tune or
Of a disease that insidiously infiltrated these pages
Bit by bit, the mist obscuring the landscape now filters
A knowledge of losing yourself falls away - crucially
At the brink, at the edge of darkness
The burst of lucidity is like a sharp flash of lightning... it
SPARKS!... CHAOS into words -
Former boundaries tell stories and impose a narrative
Time no longer slips away, like a
Cancerous cell - dividing and mutating
INSTEAD it forms a story -
Beautiful, inspiring, exhilaratingly heart - breaking...
As in the first - a recognisable expression
One now SPEAKS with one's own words
Former perspectives - move quickly to flatten
Now no sense is lost - the face, the self, no longer recedes -
No longer is gone... to a shadow -
No longer a struggle to make a meaning - one of any value
Out of the anguish, the decaying body and membrane -
From the convolutions of the brain...
The searing heat and the pounding rain...
Conspire with the light and oceans' high tide -
Out in the garden flowers begin to bloom...
The empty space once on this page -
No longer filled with absence
It's no longer filled with
Silence

LUCID DAYDREAM

I close my eyes
And in that second I dream of you
In the early morning hours
As the day enters the soul -
Surrounded by peace and quiet
The whole world sleeps
As mine is re-energised, it comes alive
Poetic
Shake dreams from your hair
Sweet Lucid Daydream
To hear my love breathe with the Ocean
To ebb and flow with the tide

MORNING

The timely interjection of night's cape
Is like an artist's bold stroke
On the canvas
Of a fading landscape
Vision is muted as darkness rolls in
UNTIL
SUNLIGHT sparks an awakening
The nocturnal - pulled under -
As Dawn breaks in,
Stealing nights thunder
The Ocean breathes with a sumptuous Blue colour
In the garden flowers bloom summer
An enlightenment of fitful illumination
Both an internal and exterior decoration
Portraits smile and hang on the wall
No longer locked in the gloom
Buried beneath the fog
In a far-off room
The night restrained and all febrile
To a revelatory existence
Of a day – no longer fragile
TO TOUCH
Reawakened limbs and put to bed old sins
With a tremendous drive
As outside the Son shines
And each 'Morning' rises with a spring

SWEETNESS & LIGHT

I've just woke up dreaming about you
Drifting in and out of consciousness…
With you
Here, there…
Everywhere
My sweetness & light
Breathing in, beginning a new day with you by my side…
Ubiquitous
On my mind…
So Beautiful
YOU

WHEN THE SKY NO LONGER CRIES

I crave your mouth, your voice, your hair.
Silent and starving, I prowl through the labyrinth visions in
my mind
You are always to be found in there,
The empty streets do not nourish me/the naked light of day
disrupts me/casting shadows on life's bitter paved walkway
I long for the synchronised measure
To waltz in side, and step in time with
the fluid rhythm of your steps.
I hunger for your physical and emotional union
to hear and share each laugh,
your eyes harvest a hunger,
the golden touch of your hand
as My mind begins to wander
I want to eat you ... devour and touch the mere surface of
your skin
The gentle softness ... pure & Natural ... each heart felt
breath within
I want to feel the sun light
undressing your body, the wholesome warmth
The sophistication and the beauty -
The class that you carry
A knowledge of mind - one that compliments mine,
I want to tease the noticeable desire, to feel the mutual
volcanic eruption
To burn in the shade of your lashes,
Pulsating, my heart beats with a pounding, it races ...
Keeping afloat in the ocean
Thumping ... deep ... in forever expansive Blue waters
Internally I'm enraptured
Eternally I am captured
Hungry - although now smiling
The twilight, for you, I give for your heart,
Come ...

As you are ...
Like a cat in the night
You shine ...
All Raven bright
I want you
Each and every night

POETRY

Nocturnal habits exacerbate
A suggestive state of mind
They lead you to attach weight and create incidents
That weren't there at the time
Take a rebel -
A mere mortal/In life
One that swims against the tide
That throws himself and plunges to the depths of the Ocean
To fight the storm, both - and to bring light
Who then seizes a diamond
With life-affirming qualities
Buried at the bottom of the Ocean, right before his eyes
Such is the obscurity
Of poetry -
A fragmentation of individuality, (like)
An outsider -
Lost in the vacuous mass of society
(Who) Appears in glory /and languishes
Under the hot Sun,
Enthused by gusts of high winds
Motivated! -
No longer deployed by Dawns decline
Or of garrulous tongue
...that forever ends in dry sentences,
But rather expresses
An artistic, imaginative
Philosophical exhibit
In which a character,
The spirit, becomes an avatar -
A stylist, a protagonist
A tragic teacher -
A maverick preacher
A hero that learns lessons in life
Through one's own failure

Poetic -
Is the playground for disaffected philosophers
Both epic and
Harmonious
Integrated with rage and with dreams of the unobtainable
A form composed and consumed by every individual
It transcends the ubiquitous personage
Inherent within the modern age
Despatching words, creating worlds
Both distinguished and refined
That unlock a greater meaning
Of revolution and disenchantment
That once clashed when combined
(And) When absorbing the chaos, clatter and clutter
Of everyday modern life

WE ARE MADE OF STARDUST

Struck by the light of the fire
The ingenious eye DREAMS in the decadence of moonlight
And puts pen to paper
In a moment of time
In which to capture the mind
All equating to the fire that burns inside
Like a fish, in a net, that is anchored
Slightly above the Ocean floor
To capture a thought
That swims - and is caught
In the flow and the stream of the subconscious
As is this -
Like a haul of groundfish
Scattered like shards
A collection of words
In letters and verse
The mind writes in form, it writes in metaphor
And of a poetic description
A parable that ionizes the condition
Using signs and symbols as instruments
That resonate in sound, using - and of all - our senses
Scribing words via an explosive pen
Translating thoughts and images directly from the head
Writing a song, in words, that sings
Billowing LOUD across the Ocean
Music is noise
Submitted to order by wisdom ...
These dreams in which we speak
Convey a place, they inscribe a landscape
In which our brains and the universe meet
They unite
And we make a connection

FLYING ON SHADOWLESS WINGS

How many faces lie hidden
Waiting for the time
When curious eyes find them?
Hidden in places
Of darkness
In which we seek secrets
Watching
As daylight disappears
And artificial street lights flicker -
Hope resides in the burning embers
Of the fire that burns inside...
Whilst flying on shadowless wings
Since the other side
Of yesterday -
Hanging on the edge of reality
Like an animal - galloping
Over the crest of the hill,
That has no rider - has no saddle
Brought to the brink of destruction/By the Devil
Where one's own existence/is both
Surreal and fantastical
Impaled - by a colourful/
Vision
That extracts a reaction
A suffusion and exploration
Of the psychological -
An abstraction, that transcends -
Like life -
And turns disaster
Into something beautiful

THE MOTHER OF INTELLIGENCE

Brave New World is neither
Brave, nor NEW,
THOUGH
It is TRUE
The suppression of WILL, and
That of others we speak ILL –
The global world devours in SUB-POCKETS,
Perpetuates dystopia and deathly ILLNESS -
Ponder the literature of SCHOLARS
In books – keep alive,
Or further the net will close in and CONTROL US
In years to come – I don't want that LIFE
Where curiosity is no longer allowed US
Maybe the MASSES
will be injecting
and drinking
heroin and hard LIQUOR
So much to OFFER,
All will be WASTED on
Mechanical cogs and tragic DIRECTIVES,
Repetition and
Repetition
PROGRAMMED to
REPETITION and
REPETITION!
THUMBS raining IN – and – OUT the INFORMATION
and DIRECTION SCREEN –
enough to make you want to
SCREAAMMM!!!!
A tale, like life, where energy fades,
Replaced by ubiquitous forms of SADISTIC STATISTICS,
Until they are replaced by yet another STATISTIC.
It is time for the CHILDREN
Of HUMANS/to take ACTION!

Teach yourself IGNORANCE
Curiosity is the Mother of INTELLIGENCE

CARPE NOCTEM

A delicate awakening
The bird chorus calls dawn in
Blue skies entice aural delights, and
Sunlight breathes in
MORNING!
The eyes - primed -
Ignite a passion within
Desire burns bright
PROJECTING
A mental and physical being
That entwines, and waltzes
Hand in hand, (and)
Glides through the nuances –
A dance that lightens up darkness
Through expressions borne of the mind
And of private dreams
That seize the night

OUT OF THE SHADOWS

Transposed
From an identity
A veil painted of complexity
That not of a dedicated monster
But that to someone familiar
In stories – of twisted and warped fantasies
Nothing but the narrator's desperate attempt to camouflage
their reality
Behind closed doors
There's nothing going on –
The lights are on
But nobody's home
Banal
Numbingly ordinary
No shocking unsettling discovery
A febrile state
In which one must question their own fears and identity
The scene from within is boring and staid
In FACT
There's nothing more to be said

THE END.

NATURE

Time echoes
Like a symphony of ghosts
That wail in the breeze
Among the Autumn trees
But then
A SMILE nestles
Dazzling Golden
On the meandering trees leaves
A delicious reflection
Hearing Nature as it Breathes!

AUTUMNAL GOLD

The view -
A vast expanse of Autumnal Gold...
Of fields, that forever unfold (and)
Naturally keep evolving
Until
Up on the horizons edge
A stream runs through
Borrowing the landscapes flow
Disturbing the ease of Green
As it breathes
Complimentary - all synchronised
With emphasised tones of Blue -
Calm, and still - the Sky
With inherent complimentary delight
Breaks on through, mid afternoon
As the Sun begins to cry
And Grey clouds gather
Surrounding days light
Intimidating - A pour sight (and)
Scouring the view -
Highlight
A vast expanse of fields, that forever unfold
And serve only to emphasise
The seasons shade of Autumnal Gold

THE DREAM OF PHILOSOPHICAL REASON

Plato speaks of truth
That of happiness and virtue
Socrates populates an ideal
In which reality is nothing but a shadow
Then on everything
Descartes casts doubt in
Precipitating a war
Between knowledge and thought
Of empiricists -
Who's existence is based around experience
Then there's the story
Of ancient Greek philosophy
Which vindicates the thinker
Towards that of Nature,
Of art - and that of society
Then rationality is pitched against novelty
With "the new idea that old ideas are suspect" -
And thus can it be argued
The I in Idea to be subjective -
The start, the foundation, of everything
Within which conjures a dream
That which philosophical reason concedes -
The theoretical, a target to be ridiculed
And as states Friedrich Nietzsche
"Man is something to be surpassed"
Just like a dream
Within which reason becomes abstract

THE STORYTELLER

Art portrays an internal landscape
An exhibition of headspace
That coincides a fascinating encounter
A miscellany of the thinker
Of confabulations that matter -
To look is to listen
An informal collage of discussion
In conversation with a writer
An incantation improvised
A summarisation of the times
A dream - A wish
A mystical desire
(Of) The storyteller
A hero with flaws
Amid textured four walls
Conjures a dream
And captures all

AN AWAKENING

Awake
My eyes grow accustomed to daylight
And sight
Armours
Itself against wonder
As I daydream
Of high deeds and intrigue
Full of wide eyes
And mystique
As Nature intervenes
At the sight - In the form - Of a sparrow
Sat perched on the sill of a window
A poignant beauty
All gregarious and noisy
As it hops - All cheerfully
And sets off flying
Among the Blue skyline, and distilled clouding
That keep on moving
Forever reforming
As I marvel at life
In all of its awe
And at all of its wonder

THE FALSE MESSIAH

Drawn like a fly
To an alluring beam
That glows
Through an open entrance
The door before is slightly ajar
Beyond
A celestial light beckons…
At the end of a dark corridor
An enticing spectacle ENLIGHTENS
But then a sudden convulsion
A dark perception
Both fierce and mordant
As the doors projection
Slams SHUT -
A shock to the system
Gale force winds blow through the Headland
Knocking purveyors of truth off their feet
Every step subsides
As the floor crumbles beneath
The vision inside - a prism of light
Echoes a piercing chorus
Of shards that SCREAM!
From a number of mirrors -
Artificial light, a shattered reflection
And of disembodied images
A symbol, a figure
Dangles from above, is
Hanging from the ceiling
One suspended in ALL its meaning
Sending tremors over and over
A feeling/Of having lost something
Like a compounding of echoes
Reverberating
With a sting in its tale (sic)

Of deep remorse
As a beautiful corpse
In a cavernous hall
Exhibits in an empty gallery
A Romanticist
That's cast adrift
Like a painting or a delicate embroidery
Completely beguiling
Nailed to the cross
Mounted
Exposed
Upon some brutal scaffolding

A JOURNEY THROUGH THE PAGES

A chilling wind blows through the frozen Headlands
Reclaiming Winter
As it clarifies the landscape
Displaying the Sky -
A serene scene,
Evoking memories of
Rustic glories
To dream a dream
And to live the story -
In multicolour and with
Everchanging vibrancy
As goes life
Passing through the seasons
Of days spent in the countryside
Watching hares leap,
Foxes hunt
And birds hiding in the hedges
Awakening Nature
Upon re-bustling
The inception of each Dawning
A chorus that builds and becomes
An iconic intensity
Portrayed in an image of tradition
The word - one, written
Is like a lone footprint
That leaves a trail
Binded and encased
Within one's journal
That's the Nature of Life -
Ensuring a preservation
An emblem
A gift
A beautiful token
Becoming one's own personal legacy

One that's captured in time
Transcending through life
And traversed throughout
The rest of history

MOURNING

The sky is grey
The clouds are pouring
Welcoming
Another wet winter mourning
In a mind scarred by landslides
The flooding is devastating
Dreams are washed away
As downpours abound outside
And so, the curtains are drawn
On all, and the world, tonight

TOUCHING FROM A DISTANCE

Seduced by melodies of drugs and booze
I've searched for clues in bedrooms
An all-out participation
That engaged my imagination
As I tried to embrace both the Sun and the Moon -
Like an anchor flung into a churning sea
I tried to look for salvation
But the consolations of poetry
Have always attracted me -
The touch of platonic purity
Replete with anguish and anxiety
Of a story that's infectious
Speaking of truth
And of a tyranny
In life, such qualities
Cast a benign spell -
They're both enduring and influential...
But...
Writing this is painful
Like extracting a nugget of wisdom -
A precious stone
A finely wrought diamond
That's cut and polished
In a suburban bedroom
In, and of,
All the quiet nights
And the solitary existence,
The tearful eye
GLISTENS
As it touches from a distance
Like a gently fulfilling love affair
Of sacred souls
And aching minds
Both fragile in their exposure -

Touching, at the brink
Whilst sinking, in
The midst of an aching existence
As is this - the pens ink
TOUCHES
Whilst skating on the surface
As the story unfolds
From a hushed scene of silence
The serenity unfurls
With a vast sense of turbulence
Emerging emphatically from the light
Is DARKNESS
With such dynamic extremity
That RIPPLES
Encircle with widespread intensity
That forever increase
Like an Ocean that's become unsettled, and THEN
Is FROZEN
Whilst two minds
Continue to
ECHO... around the ripples' trajectory
And skate
With a mutual grace
That touches perfection
And from the deepest darkest depths
Two minds collide
With such expanse
The ebb and flow of the tide subsides
And begins to breathe again a Natural rhythm
And the Sun
Continues to Burn
As it
Touches from a distance
And glistens on the surface of the Ocean

RHYTHM AND POETRY

Listen
Listen – Then listen some more
To the music's tempo, melody and chords
To the notes and words and how they're implored
In tone, and rhythm and forms –
All interpretations explored
Take Picasso dancing
With paint in hand, to throw at the wall
Each revolution represents a sensation
A projection – an evocation
That's poetic in form
A rhythm that conveys an expression,
Then with added refrain
A slip of the tongue
Just add a few words
And you're singing in song

JETTING FROM SUMMER TO WINTER

Jetting from Summer to Winter
The mind swings extraordinary
The pen ink bleeds
And is captured on sheets of white paper –
Beneath these layers on which it speaks
The mind functions
Deconstructing time
And with a flourish/ The scribe
Draws a short portrait
Of each moment –
A flash of memories,
Triggered by a smell/ One potent
Falling from above
Landing in key
An assembly of consciousness within each day
Exploring transient dreams
That merge and disperse, and
Flow in different streams
Through synchronised flashes of activity –
Writing
Whilst climbing
From one existential tree to another
Structure unfolds
Seducing the eyes of the reader -
The Narrator
EXPOSED
Strips back the mask of the day
One brimming with meaning, metaphor and ambiguity
And with a FLASH
Your mind explores
As light penetrates form
Extracting meaning from the core…
And beneath these layers
Is where subjectivity occurs

CAPTURED IN THE LIGHT OF A FALLEN MOON

Heaven – at night
ECHOES
In the light/ of a fallen moon
SHATTERED … In the distance
Filling the still streets with a pallid rejection
The CRACKED and bitter-paved walkway of life
Passes by…
As you catch a glimpse OUTSIDE,
Of each and everyone's window –
Some darkened
Some flooded…
All in shades – a full array
Of artificial light and colours faded
Presenting a carillon
A DAZZLING display
Like that of a musical instrumentation,
A set of chords from a range
One coloured
In the settling afterglow of Sunset
That represents a mindset –
One stirring with INTENSITY, before ENGULFING The
HEART
Denoting an expression
Between wonder and decay
As a duality of tension, causes an eruption
A reverberation of ECHOES
Caught in the reflection
Of each and every window
Depicting the darkness, and the loss of innocence…
CAPTURED in the SHATTERED light of Night … in the
shadow LIFE HIDES…
In the shade of a fallen moon

TONIGHT

Tonight we have the moon, and
We have the stars
They reflect in your eyes
That shine, like
Polished diamonds
Tonight we thrive
On a heart of Gold, that
Echoes deep
Whilst we sing to the sky
Of love,
In lust,
With desire

BENEATH THE EYES

The loveliness of touch
The contact, the rush
The high of simply embracing –
His hands just grazing
The edge of her translucent knickers –
Her delicate foot,
Upwardly cupped
Their naked torsos pressed together
Their legs all slender – entwined
Beneath the sky, scattered with stars
(As) They saw beneath the eyes
And freed each other
From the confinements of life

THE SOUND OF SOLITUDE

The owl is still
The night is calm... deceiving... as
Bad dreams haunt me
Night imagery
Of blood hungry wolves
In tidal waves and tornadoes
Jumping off the edge of cliffs
Committing suicide to save my life
Life burns - conduces relevance
As I burn through like a comet
Spilling talent liberally and fast - In a blaze
As the sun shines and glistens on top of a beer froth
Taking drugs
Deeper and deeper 'til I hit the bottom -
Luminous in the dark
Distorted and depressing
Self-harm and suicide
An assault of neon and electric light
The sound of solitude
Resonates
In an instant
In these shoes

SANCTIFY

The weather is sanctified
Perfect enough to diffuse the light -
A purple haze brings comfort
And solace
With a strength that enters the night...
And counting the days,
As the waves
Crash against the rocks of time and uncertainty
I contemplate the end, and
Not yet ready to surrender to its rapture
I wonder
As heaven considers
My personal affordance, with a
SILENCE
That transcends boundaries, like
An innocent kiss
That merely touches the surface... and
Anchored like a memory -
I hang forever
Between space and time...

NIGHTJAR

Within the higher echelons of the furtive mind
As with the determination to fend off the Night
Time... is slowly melting
And with the flick of a switch
Daylight encounters its 'goodbye'
Dreams become possessed with fear and emotion
As Life's passion, and drive - both
Diminish forever with desire
Just as EVERYTHING
Was in a state of becoming -
Building each day, forging a path
Bridging the gap
Between forever, and the past...
Beholding its conception/Since the beginning of time, and -
With the seal of a kiss - that's
Now been forgotten
The light begins to flicker
As we make our final wish
Goodbye.

A LULLABY IN TIME

Our blood is young and our minds are high
The bright lights roar; the sounds of the world die
Throb, stretch, thrill motion, sway... pull out and slide
Speed sharpens; grows... on, and into the night,
The strength and splendour of our purpose swings
The lamps fade; and the stars
We are alone.

In this;

A Perfect fleeting rightness of time
The moment; so delicate, and crucial as
In the mere flicker of an eye,
Night passes by ... and ... ALL vision subsides,
Not a trace in sight ... as YOU are consumed
In ALL that IS ... in ONE single moment
Recurring eternal
Trying to entice both the Sun and the Moon
An embrace that slips away and yet leaves a trail in the mind
A vibrant energy, FULL of LIFE,
That glides ... as in comes BEAUTY, she walks
With elegance and poise
She leaves a set of footsteps ...that DANCE throughout time
To the Romance of a finely tuned concerto
She waltzes ... and she conjures
A display that is swathed in beauty,
And bathed underneath the glow of EterNal moonlight
A dazzling image ... as two minds collide
And Naturally entice
As they embrace both the Sun and the Moon

ALL THOUGHTS FLICKER

(All) Thoughts flicker
Like morning Sun
That glitters on the Ocean
As sweet dreams rise up
Like shoals of fish
And kiss the surface -
All bright and all silver,
All dancing in manner
Before darting off into deeper water
Stirring shadows
Of times past and times hidden
Of times more difficult to fathom
Like solitary footsteps
Walking down a footpath
That time once had forgotten

THE LIGHT ALERT ANIMAL

The light alert animal
Take's the spotlight in one's precise imagery
She sits - exceptional
Reflective and precise
She wears her influence
In a world of art -
With Grace ... in which to entice
Eyes like the spectrum of her blended fur
As I lift her
And an animal she remains
As magic finds its release in this story
The indiminishable fact of her saliva
Her animal-ness
Takes us somewhere other
To a scene of debauchery and degradation
One where we are both involved
We both feel ...
We're on familiar ground
Like going for a long walk by the coast
Where we gain a new understanding of each other, and of
one's self
As the Sea keeps coming
Washing away, the void and the fear
White tipped and glistening
Like where the stream of the lake -
All joined, at some point -
One day, will become the stream of the Ocean
Compelling and authentic
As raw desire
Rises, and transpires
From Blue depths
And appetite is liberated in wilderness

THE WOMAN ON THE BEACH

Drifting on the edge of the shore
As the sea crashes
Against the rocks of time and uncertainty -
The downfall of Heaven continues to pour, whilst
A woman stands, alone, in the sand
Her footsteps washed away, they leave no trace
But captured, in this moment
She inspires
As she walks bare footed through the Night
with Beauty, and with Grace
Like an energy source
Amidst the crashing waves
Impervious
To the Oceans ROAR!
As the sea crashes all around us
With a SILENCE!
And in this moment
Of serene calmness
Wisdom was BORN

RIDING THE WAVES OF EMOTIONAL TURMOIL

From land to land
Crossing the Ocean
Riding the waves of human emotion
What was man -
Before words and before their invention?
And languages' subsequent conception ...
Every human - our characteristics
Has a precursor, makes us all similar
Which makes the world relative
All societies
Should have the same moral basis -
Averse to inequality
A key feature of human psychology and morality
With social systems built on reciprocity
Which in turn can be explained by the ecology ...
In human structures,
That produce and enable the occurrence of social behaviours
... Underlying processes ...
Produce multi-cultures living together
Interspersed with individuality -
Be it of vocal tone or that of one's body
And, or all, of such gestures
This nature of consciousness -
It's potential within existence, and its very presence
Is a mirror
Of self-recognition
Which imparts an inspection
On human behaviour
And rides beyond the waves of divisive turmoil and emotion

DYSTOPIA

It is the future, in the psychic centre
The air is heavy with death and decay
A mass fever of unknown etiology
Physically dark
Like that of an X-ray
An atmosphere where light is absorbed
Never reflects but sucks in its own
With surveillance systems ... data algorithms
That analyse behaviour and
Personality,
Artificial mechanisms
That are designed to make our decisions
People are tracked constantly
Our privacy
Is destroyed - along with individuality
The 21st century
Will be defined and modified by (a)
General consensus to manipulate our desires
Institutions
Such as democratic elections
Will become obsolete
As authority shifts from humans
To algorithms
Who know how to press our emotional buttons
Better than ones own Mother -
An apocalypse by shopping
An uncanny ability to try and sell us something
Philosophical problems
Political questions
Whatever happened to consciousness
And free will for the past thousands of years?
Of ethics?
To an era of life
Genetically modified and non-organic

A profound impact on our trajectory
Our future - through choice
And from the decisions we are making
Today

AN OVERTURE OF LIFE

Heavens night
Reverberates with the light ... of a full moon
Illuminating like a loyal companion
That understands what it means to be human
A chorus of echoes,
A social world where darkness governs -
It never leaves, it always watches
And no-one intrudes -
It's STEADFAST. And CONSTANT.
Knowing us in our light and dark moments
Every day is a different version of itself
Just as we - SOMETIMES are weak,
SOMETIMES we're strong
Changing every day - An awareness,
As down by the shore
You can feel forever subside
With the gentle ebb and flow of the tide
Composed.
And with a calmness -
That emanates from the closeness
Of the affluent roar
And the depths
Of yesterday's deep waters
As the sea Breathe's
With a Natural Rhythm
Of a passion/That aligns
With the moon, the stars, and the Night
Like a conductor
Directing a performance of an orchestra -
Is captured in this moment of time

With instrumentation
And the voice of a choir
That sings - full of Beauty, full of pride,
And full of wonder
As the music plays, it defines -
A scene of serenity ...
A reverberation of echoes
That rose
With a passion - and spoke
With a voice - that came
From DEEP within

PHYSICAL RESTRICTIONS

The distance strains beyond this moment
Isolation fades
After everything else has gone silent ...
Emotions ... floating
All pervading
Eerily from above
Like the words of a song
That are sung
(And make you think)
Long after the dancing is done ...
Taking the listener
Through a dizzying
Volley
Of imagery -
A despairing narrative
Of lyrics dancing on the ceiling
That intersperse
Hand-in-hand
With coherence
As is the abstraction
A distraction
From
And of this very moment

THE MAGIC OF LANGUAGE

Somewhere underneath the moon
That reclines
And smiles
Contentedly, at the world beneath
The insomniac drifts
Whilst scribbling on some sheets
And offers
A pellucid access to a great unconscious
That's fascinating ...
Shape-shifting
Like the road before, that stretches
To a place that heads off into the wildness
And writes some lines
Which, in itself, is an adventure
Enticing
Like an enigmatic complexity
That captures the subject perfectly
With an idiosyncratic gaze
That's scribed upon the page
Capturing the heat
Hectic - subjective
Very much alive
Yet cool and serene
Beautiful and sublime
Absolutely captivating
That always arrives
A hauntingly, beautiful, mesmerising tale
Delicate and thoughtful
Dense and concise
With playful rhythms
That project and unite
Against the power and madness of a class that divides
With a mentality
Courting catastrophe

Whilst writing ... tempting a book
That one was born to write
With a warmth
That represents a truth
Of a light
That will never go out -
That's the magic
Of language -
It transcends ... like the moon -
Coloured and soaring
And always in flight

HOWL

(And) As imagination bodes forth
Breaking through FORM
And penetrates vision
Banging down on veiled walls
As Night submits
To sweet lullabies
And you hear the cries of Naked submission
Until - All hysterical
Sunlight caresses the body
An encapsulation
That SINGS all Golden
A cacophony of HOWLS
With eyes primed wide open
That SCREAM of absolution
As the Devil's Delight
And gorge upon
The mind
And it's total consumption

AD METAM

INDEX